The Best of
The Lemonhe

MW00682466

Amsco Publications
New York • London • Paris • Sydney

All photographs by Jesse Peretz

This book Copyright © 1995 by Amsco Publications
A Division of Music Sales Corporation, New York

Order No. AM 92050
US International Standard Book Number: 0.8256.1407.4
UK International Standard Book Number: 0.7119.4180.7

Exclusive Distributors:
Music Sales Corporation
257 Park Avenue South, New York, NY 10010 USA
Music Sales Limited
8/9 Frith Street, London W1V 5TZ England
Music Sales Pty. Limited
120 Rothschild Street, Rosebery, Sydney, NSW 2018, Australia

Printed in the United States of America by
Vicks Lithograph and Printing Corporation

ALISON'S STARTING TO HAPPEN

BY EVAN DANDO

Moderately fast
(muted guitar strings)

(Half-time feel on repeat)

1. She'd shake it up,____ Was hard____ to make__ out. Now__

2. *See additional lyrics*

____ it's plain to see____ I could-n't cook to save__ my-self,__

____ Found my life____ a rec-i-pe.____ I ne-ver

looked at her__ this way be-fore,__ But now she's all I

see._____ Al-i-son's start-ing to hap-pen, Al-

i-son's start-ing to hap-pen, Al-i-son's start-ing to hap-

8

the couch, ___ made the sky ___ com - plete. _____

Al - i - son's start - ing to hap - pen. Al - i - son's start - ing to hap-

pen. Al - i - son's start - ing to hap - pen. Al-

i - son's start - ing to hap - pen. Al - i - son's get - ting her tit ___

___ pierced. Al - i - son's grow - ing a mo - hawk. Al-

i - son's start - ing to hap - pen to me. ___

Additional lyrics

2. It's so mesmerizing, can't describe it,
    All that inside, hey.
    No one's heard her last name, I ain't asked,
    So who am I to blame?
    An earthquake started boiling underneath my feet today.

A CIRCLE OF ONE
BY EVAN DANDO

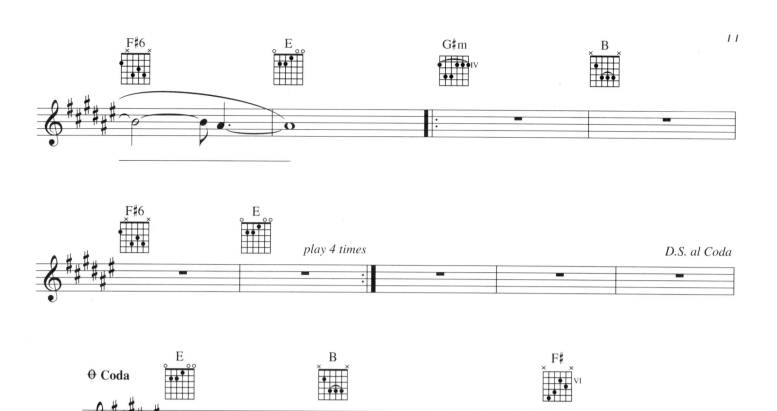

play 4 times

D.S. al Coda

Coda

BEING AROUND
BY EVAN DANDO AND TOM MORGAN

Moderately fast

1. If I was in the
2., 3. *See additional lyrics*

fridge would you o- pen the door?_____

If I was the grass_____ would you mow_____ your lawn?__

If I was your bod - y would you still__

__ wear clothes?__ If I was a boog-

er would you blow_____ your nose?__ Where would you keep__

__ it? Would you eat_____ it? I'm just tryin' to give my-self a rea-

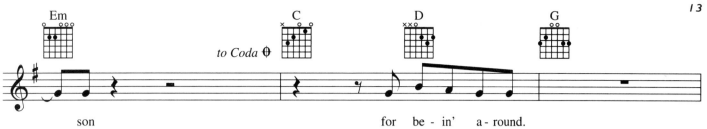

son   for be - in' a - round.

1.

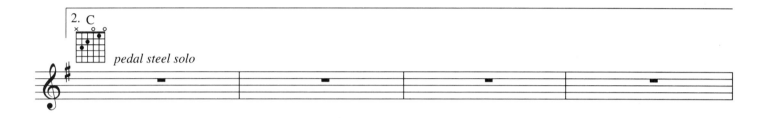

2. C

pedal steel solo

D.S. al Coda

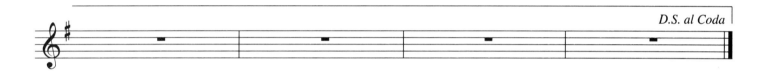

⊕ **Coda**

I'm a lit - tle grub- by   just be - in' a- round.__

Additional lyrics

2. If I was a front porch swing would you let me hang?
    If I was a dance floor would you shake your thing?
    If I was a rubber check would you let me bounce up
        and down inside your bank account?
    Would you trust me not to break you?
    I'm just tryin' really hard to make you notice me
        being around.

3. If I was a haircut would you wear a hat?
    If I was a maid could I clean your flat?
    If I was the carpet would you wipe your feet in time to
        save me from mud off the street?
    If you like me, if you loved me would you get down on
        your knees and scrub me?

DAWN CAN'T DECIDE

BY EVAN DANDO AND NIC DALTON

1. Dawn can't de-cide___
2.,3. *See additional lyrics*

___ if there should be more of the porch,___ she's sick___ of be-ing___

___ in - side. He read the signs___

___ and now they're mak - in' out in Lan - cast - er___ just to

pass the time. Woo!

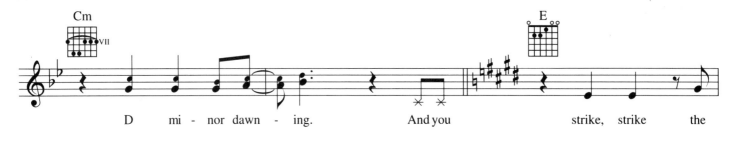

D mi - nor dawn - ing. And you strike, strike the

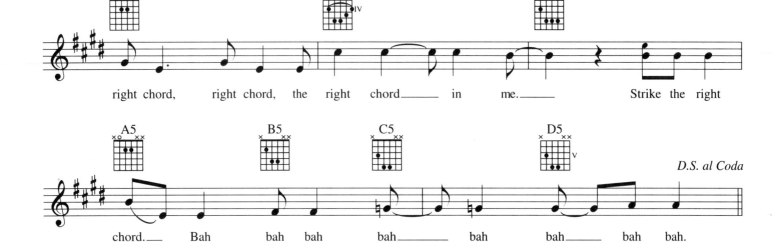

right chord, right chord, the right chord____ in me.____ Strike the right

D.S. al Coda

chord.____ Bah bah bah bah____ bah bah____ bah bah.

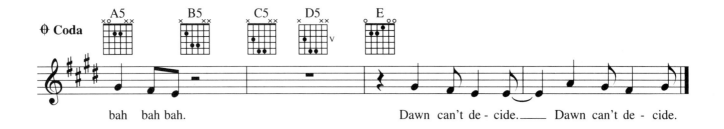

⊕ Coda

bah bah bah. Dawn can't de - cide.____ Dawn can't de - cide.

Additional lyrics

2. Curtis C called.
   Left a message in Japanese.
   Dawn took the call.
   Reviewed the newest Taang! release.
   Joe shudda known that the Long Island Lolita would be the cause.

3. Bah bah bah bah
   Bah bah bah bah bah, bah bah, bah bah bah bah bah.
   No paperwork.
   No paperwork.
   bah bah bah bah
   bah bah bah bah bah, bah bah, bah
   bah bah bah bah.

DIE RIGHT NOW
BY EVAN DANDO

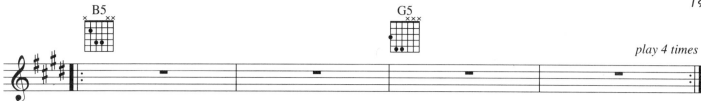

play 4 times

(spoken):
*And then I went to the end of it, and the old man, well, he's ready to die. And he said,
"Well, Tom, sincerity's the best gimmick. Remember that." And I say, "All right, be
sincere, that'll win it?" He said, "That's it. Sincerity and honesty," he said, "will do it.
It'll trick'em every time." I said, "Well, sincerity and honesty; I never tried that."*

D.S. al Coda

with Rhythm figure 1 *simile*

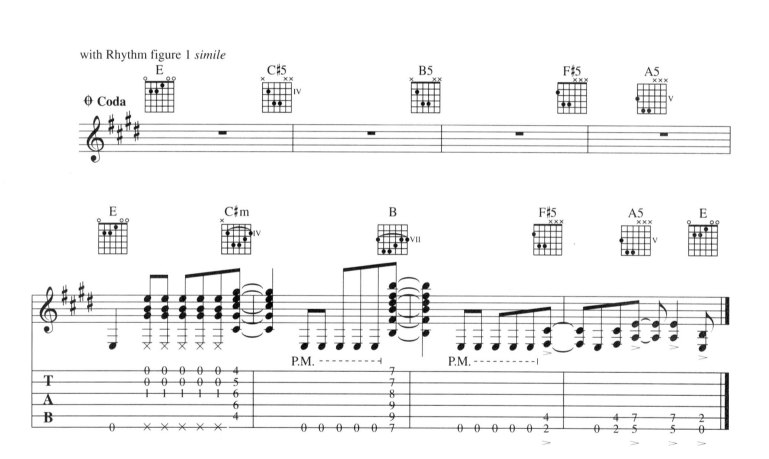

DON'T TELL YOURSELF IT'S OK
BY EVAN DANDO

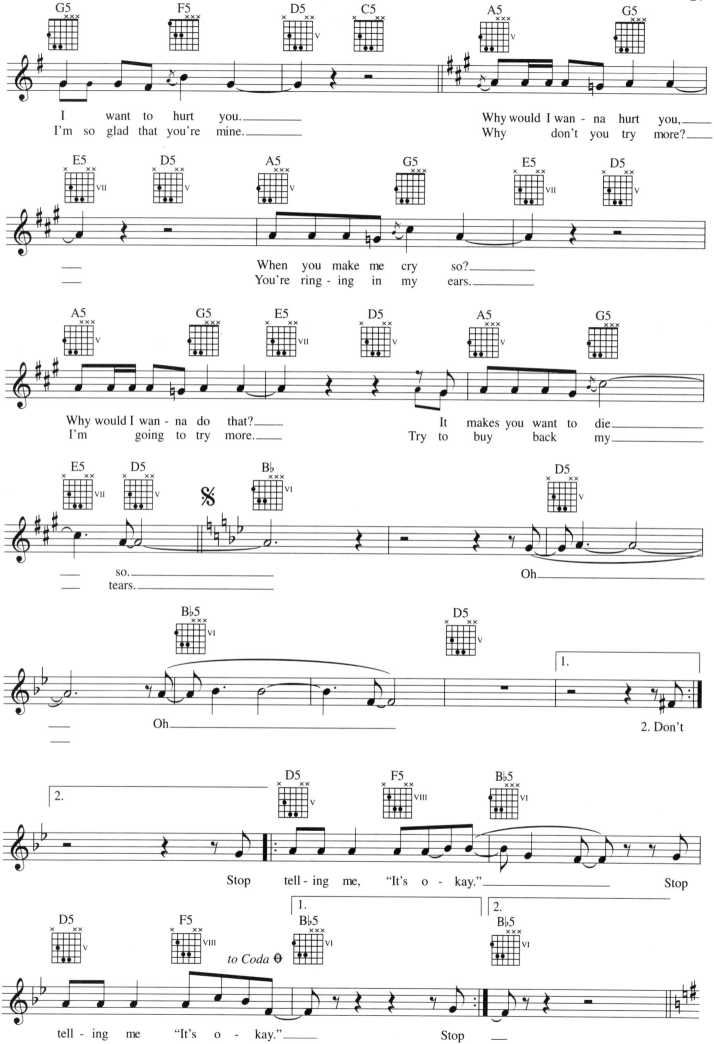

IT'S A SHAME ABOUT RAY

BY EVAN DANDO AND TOM MORGAN

Moderately

1. I've nev-er been____ too good____ with names.____
2. *See additional lyrics*

The cel-lar door_____ was o-pen, I_____ could nev-er stay____

_____ a-way._____ I know it's prob-'ly not____ my place.

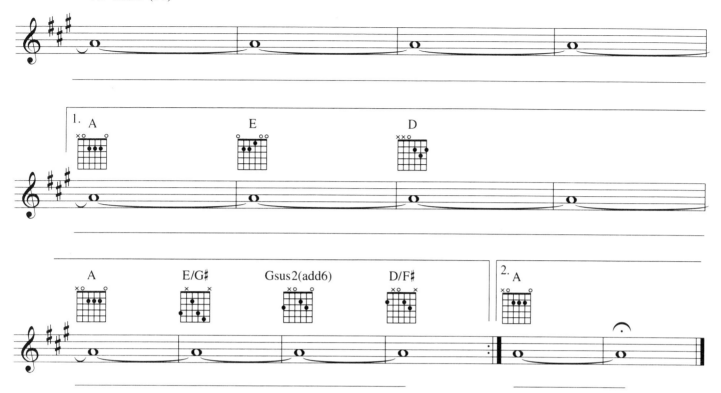

Additional lyrics

2. If I make it through today,
   I'll know tomorrow not to leave my feelings out on display.
   I'll put the cobwebs back in place.
   I've never been too good with names but I remember faces.

GLAD I DON'T KNOW

BY EVAN DANDO

Moderately fast

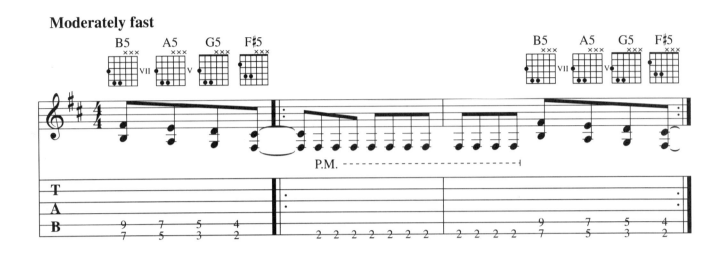

1. I'm glad_____ I don't

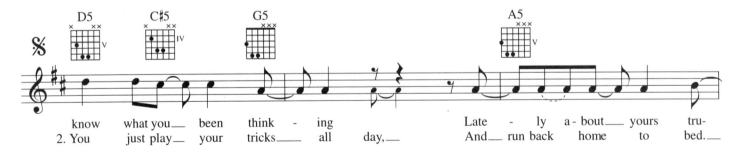

know what you_ been think - ing
2. You just play your tricks___ all day,___ And run back home to bed.___
Late - ly a - bout_ yours tru -

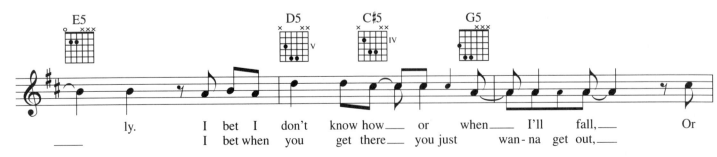

ly. I bet I don't know how___ or when___ I'll fall,___ Or
___ I bet when you get there___ you just wan - na get out,___

HALF THE TIME
BY EVAN DANDO

Moderate

HATE YOUR FRIENDS

BY EVAN DANDO

hate your friends.   You   hate your friends.   You

hate your friends

play 4 times

THE GREAT BIG NO

BY EVAN DANDO AND TOM MORGAN

MY DRUG BUDDY

BY EVAN DANDO

1. She's com-in' o - ver, we'll go out walk - ing, Make a call_ on the way.
2. *See additional lyrics*

She's in the phone_ booth now,_ I'm look-in' in._

There _ comes a smile _ on her face.

There's still some of the same stuff we got yes - ter - day. _

There's still some of the same stuff we got yes - ter - day, _ yeah. _

to Coda ⊕

I'm

too much with my - self, I _ wan - na be some - one else. I'm

too much with my - self, I _ wan - na be some - one else. I'm _

D.S. al Coda

too much with my - self, I wan - na be some - one else. 2. So we take

⊕ Coda

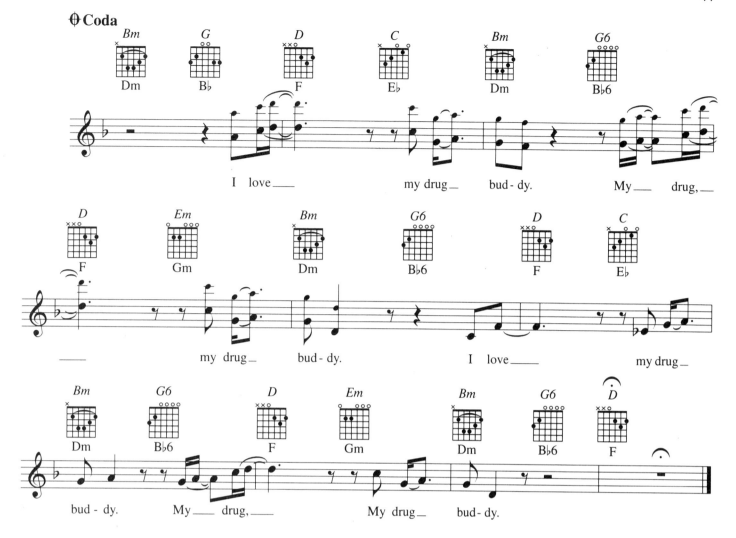

I love___ my drug_ bud-dy. My___ drug,___
___ my drug_ bud-dy. I love___ my drug_
bud-dy. My___ drug,___ My drug_ bud-dy.

Additional lyrics

2. So we take off out Fiona's door,
   Walk until it's light outside,
   Like before when we were on the phone.

   We have to laugh to look at each other.
   We have to laugh 'cause we're not alone.

   As the cars fly up King Street
   It's enough to startle us,
   It's enough to startle us.

   (to Coda)

LEFT FOR DEAD

BY EVAN DANDO

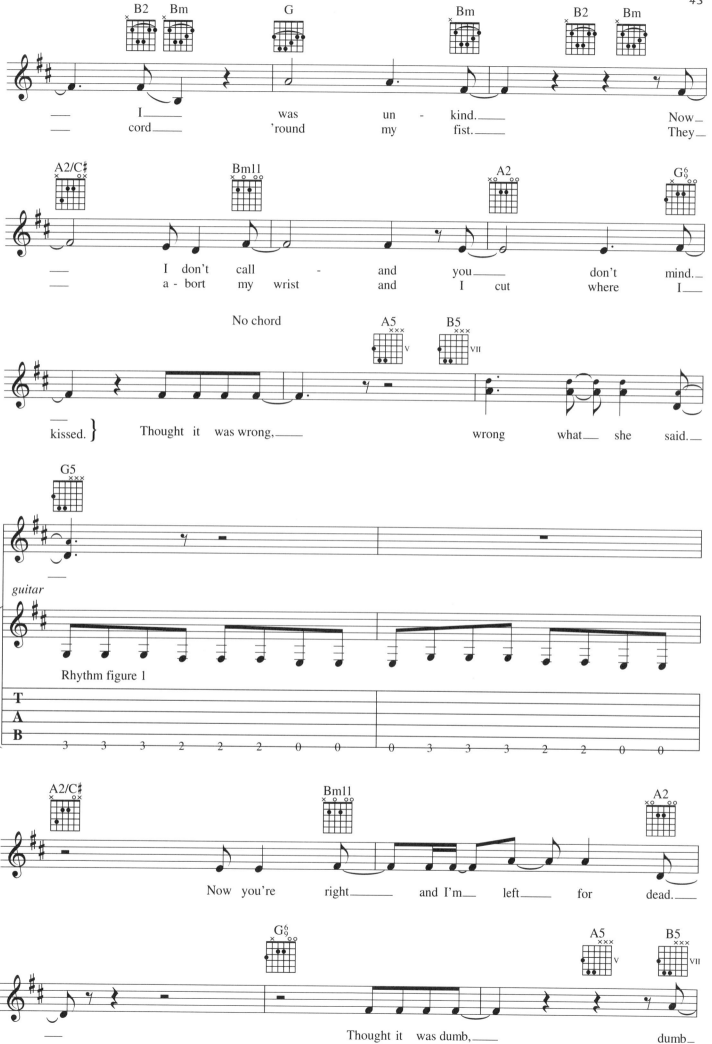

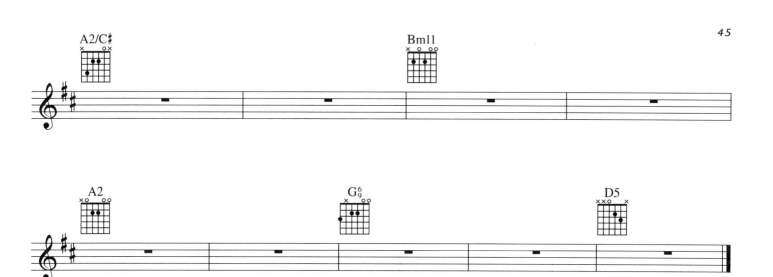

MALLO CUP

BY EVAN DANDO

Moderately fast

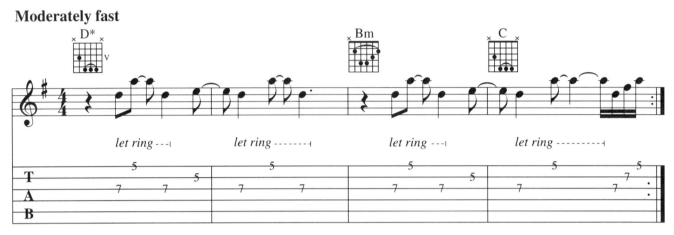

* Harmony implied by bass

1. Here I am_____ out-side your house_____ at 3 A. M._____
2. And you saw_____ noth-ing_____ in my_____ eyes but your-self._____

Try'n to think_____ you out_____ of bed._____
Noth-ing_____ in my_____ eyes._____

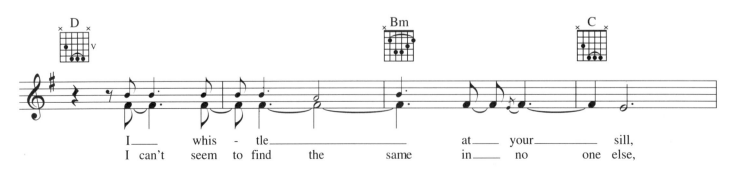

I_____ whis-tle_____ at_____ your_____ sill,
I can't seem to find the same in_____ no one else,

⊕ **Coda**

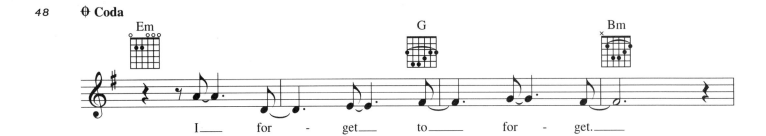

I___ for - get___ to___ for - get.___

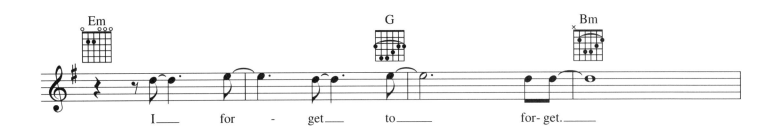

I___ for - get___ to___ for- get.___

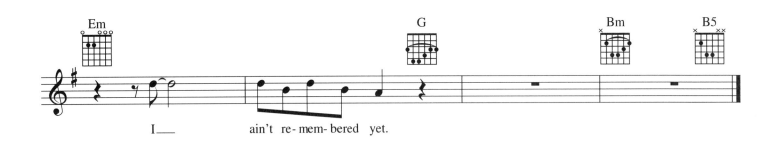

I___ ain't re-mem-bered yet.

RIDE WITH ME

BY EVAN DANDO

1. That pen - cil smell
2. He's eve - ry-where.
3. *guitar solo*

re - minds me of school.
Sends me straight 'cross the plain.

The clock on the wall
He's in your hair.

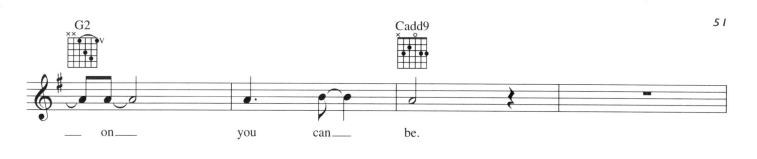

on__ you can__ be.

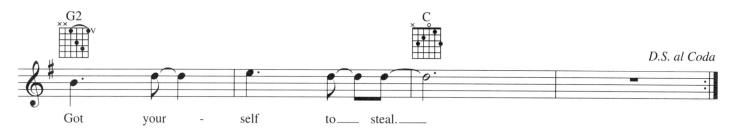

D.S. al Coda

Got your - self to__ steal.__

θ **Coda**

Ride with me.__ Ride__

__ with__ me.__ Ride_____ with__

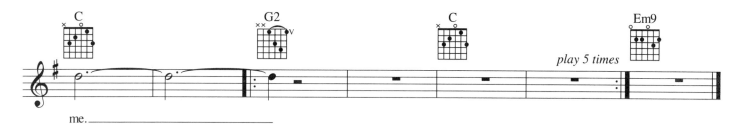

play 5 times

me.__

BY EVAN DANDO

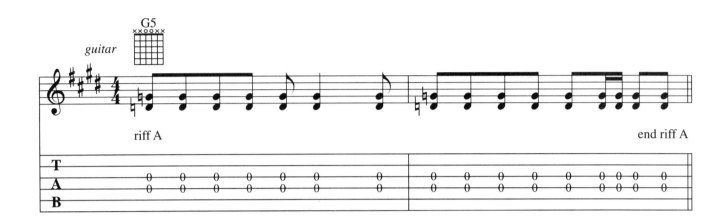

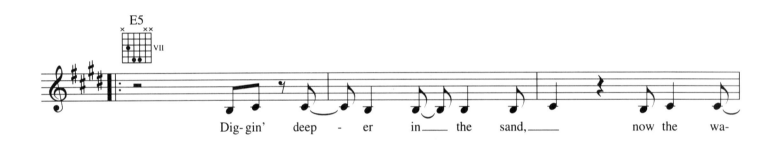

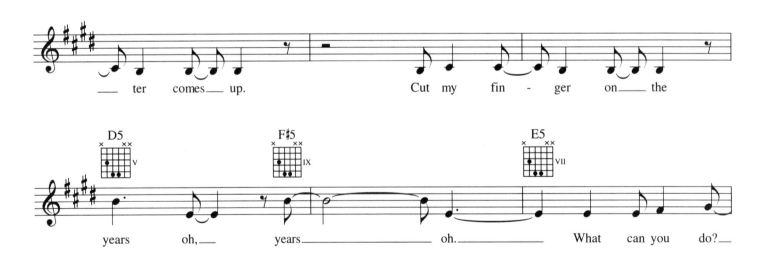

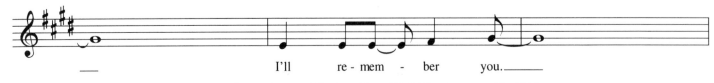

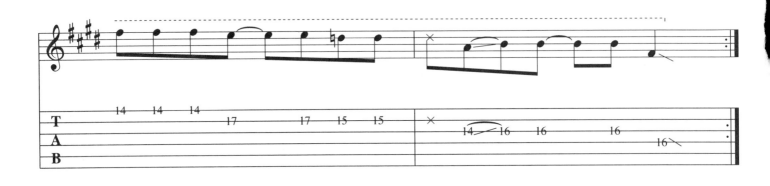

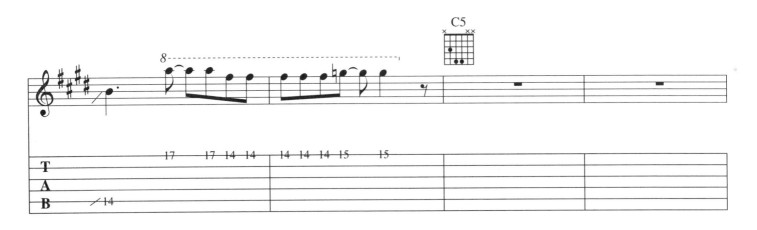

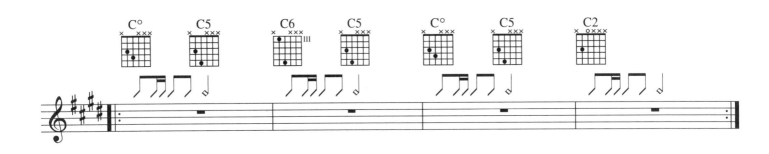

ROCKIN' STROLL
BY EVAN DANDO

56

Additional lyrics

2. Looking upward to the sky,
   Moving forward all the time.
   The sidewalk lines, "gadunk-gadunk-gadunk-gadai."
   If it's warm in here, is it cold down there?
   Around out where I can only stare.
   I'm still aware of little, but I'm gonna try.

STOVE
BY EVAN DANDO

Half-time feel

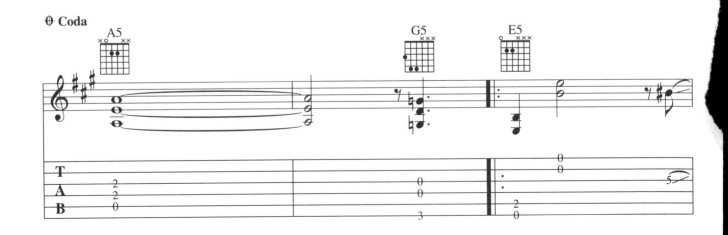

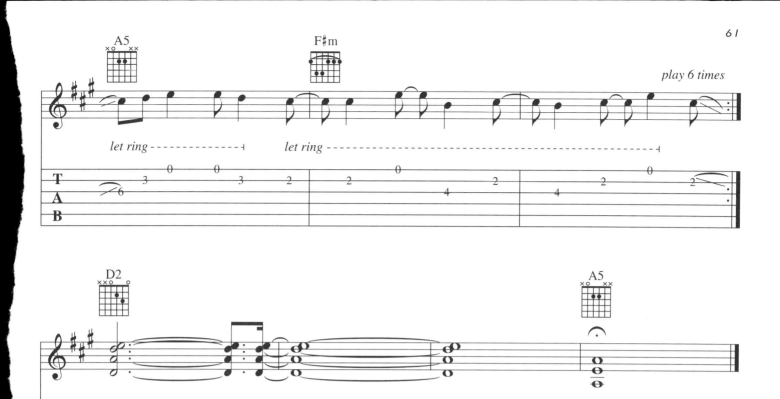

SAD GIRL
BY EVAN DANDO

sad   girl.____

steady gliss